We Are In Danger of Drowning

poems by

Loren Moreno

Finishing Line Press
Georgetown, Kentucky

We Are In Danger of Drowning

For my mother, Debbie Pinho.

Copyright © 2018 by Loren Moreno
ISBN 978-1-63534-394-6 First Edition
All rights reserved under International and Pan-American Copyright Conventions. No part of this book may be reproduced in any manner whatsoever without written permission from the publisher, except in the case of brief quotations embodied in critical articles and reviews.

ACKNOWLEDGMENTS

Thank you to the following publications where some of these poems first appeared.

The American Poetry Journal (At the Top of the Stairs)
Hawaii Pacific Review (In Every House, a Shadow Beyond the Door)
Haunted Waters Press (All Those Seagulls)
JMWW (Eel Fishing, Fireflies in Union Square Sound Like Your Father)
Olentangy Review (Jonah Falls in Love with a Tree, For Jonah's Mother)
decomP (When All the Lights Go Out)

Publisher: Leah Maines
Editor: Christen Kincaid
Cover Art: Rosa Palma/Pixabay
Author Photo: Photo by David Croxford/*Honolulu Magazine*
Cover Design: Elizabeth Maines McCleavy

Printed in the USA on acid-free paper.
Order online: www.finishinglinepress.com
also available on amazon.com

Author inquiries and mail orders:
Finishing Line Press
P. O. Box 1626
Georgetown, Kentucky 40324
U. S. A.

Table of Contents

Prelude
Eel Fishing, Leahi Beach

I. Water
Jonah Boards a Ship 1
Jonah Enters a Fish 2
Memory in a Marina 3
At the Top of the Stairs 6
Jonah in a Bath Tub 7
She Fought With Dad and Tossed the Car Key Out
    the Window 8
Sunday School Jonah Villanelle 10
For Jonah's Mother 11
After the Sailors Threw Jonah Overboard 12

II. Vapor
Jonah's Lyric in the Fish 14
Transubstantiation 15
All Those Seagulls 19
Fireflies in Union Square Sound Like Your Father 20
In Every House, a Shadow Beyond the Door 21
Self-Portrait of America as Nineveh 22
Forty Days of Fasting 23
Jonah Falls in Love with a Tree 25
When All the Lights Go Out 26
Can We Go Back to the Time Before Fire 27

Postlude
At the Site of Jonah's Burial

Prelude

Eel Fishing, Leahi Beach

Could I ever convince you to go back
to that night sitting on the rock wall jutting out
into the Pacific? Diamond Head's old man face
watching us wait forever for tugs on our line,

a signal that we've caught that elusive lightning
hidden away in the crevices of the rocks.
A summer sky blends into water.
Beneath us tiny phosphorescent fish,

with their night vision, make their way
to the edge of the Earth, back to the constellations.
We eat cherries, spitting out poison-filled pits.
Turning our faces toward the mists off the ocean,
we talk about everything but—

God dials down the knob on the night
and the stars brighten. Then a jingle bell signal:
We finally catch one, its skinny whirling dervish dance
all silvers and greens. Contain it to a bag and hang

it from the rocks. We strip the clothes off
our bodies, jumping into the water. A rush
of ripples surges out across the sea,
our message, unbottled, to a bedridden world.

The bag on the rocks, it's wriggling, violently,
as if it contains a million moaning stars. The eel,
restless in its captivity, eventually reels
itself free
        (and after all that waiting).
We intended to let it go, though, didn't we?
But what else did we lose, without meaning to?

I. Water

> *"Have you built your ship of death, O have you?"*
> —D.H. Lawrence

Jonah Boards a Ship
> *"But Jonah rose to flee to Tarshish from the presence of God."*
> —*Jonah 1:3*

The wind that cries
to the perishable parts of us.

I am no one
he should know.

I am a son who flees—
the first time in my life
without keys to a home.

Aboard, headed abroad,
even a storm cannot keep me
from being a figure
in someone else's dream.

What does it mean to hear
voices in your sleep
(mother's songs, father's screams),
like a course in memory—

to sit outside the facade of yourself,
to see your wounds,
how they bloom in the dark?

We are in danger of drowning.

This ship, hull, stern and ballast—
it will not take long
for the wind to penetrate
the inner parts of us.

Call to your god, they say.

This storm, these gusts of wind—

He is calling to *me*.

Jonah Enters a Fish

I cannot remember the way
you taught me to tie a fishing line,
a dependable knot.

Though my body is mine,
these hands are your hands
pierced & weeping.

I stand at the end of a rock wall,
cast a line to sea
as the horizon disappears, a sky exploding.

Disappointment, an overflowing ocean,
boats run aground past our stilted house,
& children pushing stranded seals back to sea.

The wind that whistles
sand into patterns,
spelling out the names of the dead.

I'll paddle out a half a mile
to the outer reef, fast & hard—
believing it to be the way to you.

I'll enter the belly of a fish.
Inside it I'll forget dry land & your face.
Inside it I'll wait three years for the sun

to rise at the horizon of its tongue.

Memory in a Marina

Think of memory as reconstruction,
each time reassembling the bricks of a moment,
each time the memory a slightly degenerated
resemblance to actual events.

This unreliability of memory,
which is why he has chosen not to tell this story,
allowing instead an omniscient narrator
to piece together a non-adaptive version:

Small boats tottering in the marina,
a mother leading her five-year old
son into an arcade by the hand for a birthday party.
    The name of the arcade is omitted
        because of its association with men
                                    in costumes.
Would it matter if his mother
        was a depressed, and often he'd watch
her take too many pills?
It shouldn't.

        A kidnapping—
a man luring away this doughy
little thing from a game of skee ball.
        A leathery hand and he reaches out
to grab it. Maybe the boy saw
in the man's hand something of
                            his father?
Another boy in a panic.

Slow down, think through your words.

A confection of melody over loud speakers
interrupted for an announcement:

*Three-feet tall, black hair, wearing denim shorts
and a red shirt, a boy has gone—
Last seen with a man, about six-feet tall,
black hair, tattered brown shirt, denim pants.*

The mother's scream is terrifying.
Other mothers scramble for their
own children, seeing in their minds
a black hole   milk cartons   afternoon specials.

Employees remove furry animal heads.
They go through the motions: *This again?*

Police find the boy and the man inside
a bathroom of a burger chain in the same strip mall
overlooking the marina of bobbing boats.

The man—
he's zipping up a dress,
applying lipstick.

Can you believe it? Lipstick!

Greased up kids and bewildered parents
look on as the man in a dress, cuffed, is pushed
into a squad car and driven away.

Now grown, he holds a few key images, only
tried telling the story once
to a lover, and he was met with a cadavers' stare.

That's incredible.
As in, lack of credibility.
As in, impossible to believe.

It has led him to question,
to see the story unfold in different ways.

Is this the nature of memory:
reshaping the past
to spare others discomfort,
ourselves shame?

At the Top of the Stairs

Without you this house is a damp dark thing.
August's humid air seeps through windows,
stench from an unclean mouth.

Orange carpet fades to jaundice,
squares of overripe tangerine remain
where furniture stood.
Though he is not here, a gripping
infiltrates the atmosphere like a held breath.

I sense the delicate line you straddled:
Let him be, after he found me behind a dresser
playing dolls with the neighbor boy.

Boys dance, too. Haven't you heard of Baryshnikov?
After he caught me wearing yellow tulle
with the neighbor boy's sister.

I have come to retrieve a relic, some small token
of forgotten fondness between you and me.

I reach the top of the stairs. An apparition:
I am 15 years younger
a bruise, blue and blotched
like an abandoned sparrow's egg.

This old me, clutching
a plastic doll stripped of its clothes.
Let go of the doll. Let it go.

Jonah in a Bath Tub

No lake, toy boat, toy Loch Ness creature.
Where did the gray whale go?
Will you turn out the lights? Let's mimic

the night sky. This water too still—
too warm, too quiet, too white to fear.
Toy boy falls through foam from the boat.

The eater of Jonah floats near—
see him lifting his pale gray head,
the terrible egg of an unborn devil.

Three days are too few for this story.
Should we kill the crew?
Who will be the voice of God?

She Fought With Dad and Tossed the Car Key Out the Window

He approaches—
a tall shadow,
like a man on stilts.

Hurry, sister,
find the key.
How long can the wind
keep him back?

Road through sugar cane,
rain slow.

He calls your name
like a slap, a belt snap—
his voice odd even to wind.

White dress,
night's untamed hair.
In the distance
he strikes a match,
illuminates his face
& the field's leaves
clatter, begging—
as if fire were water.

Sister, are you scared?
Or are we on our knees
like Golgotha pilgrims
sifting for relics—

You outgrew
the white dress.
Do you know how I took it
like burial linen,
held it to my boy body?

What am I?
That I let him drive away
& you walked
the gravel road home alone?

Sunday School Jonah Villanelle

was it a magic fish, or a kind of whale
how did he get in there
he musta been the size of a snail

did the pirates die, or keep sailing
they weren't pirates, stupid
was it a magic fish, or a kind of whale

my mom only cooks fish when it's on sale
what did it smell like in there
he musta been the size of a snail

he shoulda dug his way out with his nails
what happened to the pirates though
was it a magic fish, or a kind of whale

I would have put the pirates in jail
or fed them to a shark or a whale
their hearts must be the size of snails

what is it with you and pirates, Dale
        because they almost killed someone—
was it a magic fish, or a kind of whale
he musta been the size of a snail

For Jonah's Mother

Your house built on stilts,
shore erosion threatens to consume it.

God is the flashlight you held
as you scoured the beach
for your disappeared son—
you called it hope.

The moon mirrors your blue hue.
I am standing in the nervous light of you.

Four children, yet you are alone.
No one writes anymore. No one
draws you pictures.

Your youngest, this boy obsessed
with water has left you.
This is the story as you know it—
kidnapped by sailors
in search of sea monsters.

Your husband tries to convince you
that your children never existed.
To think you made them up.

In your bone-colored night gown
up to your knees in ocean,
God has never been further.

You shine your light
over the black canvas
of the Atlantic, as if painting—

creating your son anew,
imagining all the ways he will die,
no use in praying that he will live.

After the Sailors Threw Jonah Overboard
"Then they cried 'Please, do not let us perish for taking this man's life.'" —Jonah 1:14

  the night   the fog
     the wind almost a gale

   the vessel & its sail
      bellowed into pieces

 a rain that erodes the soul

 we listen to the oars
    knifing the ocean into waves

     feel our hearts
       grow fainter

 our water-wrinkled hands
      longing for dry land

   surely warmth will find us

    in this too small abyss
   our frail minds bend new lies

 the night   the fog
    the wind almost a gale

   the lack of knowledge
     that we were perishing

II. Vapor

"And what of the dead? They lie without shoes in their stone boats." —Anne Sexton

Jonah's Lyric in the Fish
> *"Jonah prayed to God from the belly of the fish." —Jonah 2:2*

I.

only silence penetrates the flesh \ a darkness night will never know
my call to you unheard in my distress \ only silence penetrates the flesh
in this womb, just one success— \ how my longing to hear you grows
in the silence that penetrates the flesh \ a darkness only I will ever know

II.

why cast me into the deep \ enveloped like an egret in an egg
what use in exile to eat, to sleep \ why cast me into the deep
make promises I cannot keep \ a memory of you & I wail, beg
O, I am cast into the deep \ an egret with no wings, no legs

III.

the thinnest thread of light \ the briefest glimpse of your face
could save me. I'd hold tight \ to the thinnest thread of light
& knit a tapestry of the night \ sky. surely my work to enlace
the thinnest thread of light \ will earn me a glimpse of your face

Transubstantiation

1. Take, eat. This is my body.

Don't you just get tired?
    All this talk about what naked feels like, when we
could just be naked. Why the ontological meltdown?
                Then when I'm naked,
    I'm forced to guess what you're thinking at the sight of this,
          my body, scarred from surgeons' signatures carved
into my skin.
    I'm sorry that I nearly died and needed resuscitation,
        tubes stabbed between ribs to drain the blood
            that filled my lungs.

We could turn out the lights. I could lie on my side.
                        Maybe close your eyes?

    Even Christ, pierced through the ribs,
though I realize he wasn't a sexual being
                (another ontological argument).

2. Drink this, all of you. This is my blood.

This is the age of anxiety, and I am a cat, emotionally,
                              clawing my way up the drapes
        (and afraid of water).

Your curiosity about my feet, misshapen.
                                (Don't you just get tired?)
                I'll blame it on my father.
        Either that, or a story of a toddler-size me
                        running through a heap of hot coals,
        those glowing red eyes,
discarded on the beach
        (the same beach where I would almost drown).

Seems the story of my life is near-deaths.
                                Such is the world, drowning in blood.

3. For the forgiveness of sins.

Dear Grandma, dear photograph
        of you fully dressed and
                standing in the sand.
    Dear swimmers, dear boats, dear surfers
        you saw that day.
How long had it been
        since you'd seen a beach?
    Dear painting of Jesus praying in Gethsemane,
                dear Christ on the cross,
        tell me I haven't really sinned against you,
    tell me you can wash me clean
                with the water I am so afraid of.
Dear Grandma, dear photograph
        of you fully dressed and
                standing in the sand,
    there is so much I want to tell you.
Will you go to the beach with me?
                        We can wear our clothes.

4. Do this in remembrance of me.

Thomas Merton's solution to desire for flesh:
                    meditate on the body as a corpse.

They cut the heels off her shoes to fit them on her feet.
       My grandma, lying in wake, her skin hardened
from the formaldehyde.
            Nothing about her, except silver hair, did I recognize.
       My grandpa says, *She looks just the way she did*
when she was thirty years old.

          Do not mutilate me.
               Do not keep me in this body you can barely look at.

I imagine myself as dust
       pulverized bits of bone
(flesh and these scars melted in the inferno)
            and you will plunge your hands into an urn of me
grab handfuls of this, my body,
       to scatter into the ocean I always feared.

All Those Seagulls

I found on the shelf the last book
your mother read. The dog-eared pages
marked with her marginalia.

Tell me again about the face we saw in the window,
blossoming like a blotch of ink from a fountain pen,
how you thought it was your mother's.

In the mornings when the dead don't rise
we substitute them
with artificial light.
Or else a photograph of her in La Jolla with all those seagulls,
or her voicemail still saved on my phone.

No one is interested in reality, anymore.
The seminarian in me somehow knows
what she means.
                Except, when you looked into the face
of your dying mother did you see the image of God?

Your first reaction was to crawl in bed with her,
cradle her breathless body and press your face to her skin.
Do you remember all this? Tell me and I'll show you
the margin where she wrote,
                        Memory! Memory!

Tell me again how you looked into her eyes
and saw all those seagulls
landing on the backs of seals lying on the rocks.

Fireflies in Union Square Sound like Your Father

Whole skyscrapers. Glittering monuments
to my own ineptitude I could build and still
never satisfy you.

Not even these stars
streaking through the sky,
or a holy ritual as an altar boy I rehearsed for your sake
(though I didn't believe in your religion),
with ceaseless benedictions curling upward in smoke
from a swung thurible in a serpentine litany—
still you'd find fault.

Tonight I sit in this park,
and overhear the word *enthralled*,
picture the young and old faces
of those I loved who could never love me back.

A bronze Washington is riding off to war, again.
I hardly believe what I see: a flood of fireflies
lift off a branch, a ghost, perfect
in its strangeness, singing in that familiar paternal voice,
your song of *not good enough*.

In Every House, a Shadow Beyond the Door

> *"It can last from a few seconds to a minute or two and is often associated with hypnogogic hallucinations, things you see when you're trying to wake up."*
> —Dr. Priyanka Yadav

The doorway, rectangle cut in the peeling white wall,
opens to blackness, where the mind superimposes
shapes and figures emerging from nothing.

I awake in night sweats, attempt to make meaning
from what I think I see beyond the frame.
Nothing? Nothing.

("People often see someone coming into their room—
they're not able to move or talk or scream or anything.")

As a child, I believed I saw the outline of a man
ambling like a prisoner of war across the living room—
No way to get to my father's gun in the drawer.

Tonight, the burning rope twists inside. The walking,
the shadow there beyond the door. You are beside
me, and I thumb the scar down the center of your chest.

The shadow comes to rest, stops at the door, speaks
by swapping out images in my thoughts—
Can I reveal them to you? Rusted bike. Dirt path

through sugar cane. Abandoned house. My father
aiming at a door. A shadow? A glare? Just for fun?
Just for fun. This is my rifle. This is my gun.

Self-Portrait of America as Nineveh
    After Anne Sexton

    "God said to Jonah, 'Set out for the great city of Nineveh, and announce to it the message that I will tell you.'" —Jonah 3:2

We are America,
the latched room
where the kidnapped are kept.
We are the captor—
we indoctrinate, we are masters
at the art of liberation.

Missiles sail into arid land.
We call it mercy.
They bloom like Easter lilies
that die slow then all at once.
Come, children,
we want to shackle you
to the basement wall
and suffocate your religion.
Don't worry for your mothers.
We have a separate room
where we pile the bodies.
You're going to love us.
You're going to love

the bloody fist of America,
of the butcher dressing meat,
hanging it from hooks in the window.

Jonah & Forty Days of Fasting
> *"The Ninevites believed Jonah's warning. A fast was proclaimed, and all of them, from the greatest to the least, put on sackcloth and ashes." —Jonah 3:5*

Everything violent
that enters the heart
defiles from within.

We observed his disciples
how they did not eat
how they waited
at the edge of the woods
gaunt and dour
their palates whet
at the sight of a rabbit grazing.

Hunger, the primitive desire.

This must be a test:
The Teacher
who stations his students
near ashen trees—

their cracked lips envious
of a deer drinking
at the water brook in the distance.

*Normal behavior
of the starving
is violence.*

Look, a line of geese, smallest to biggest—
then restraint.

How long can one sustain
such emptiness?

With their lips, their hearts,
they cling to God.

They shall die
dedicated to God.

Jonah Falls in Love With a Tree

> *"Then God provided a plant. And when it grew up over Jonah's head he was greatly delighted with it." —Jonah 4:6*

you longed to be loved
so I whispered about water
you longed for the hum of birds
so I fathered your flowers

we are one flesh
take any part of me you need

pry my eyes from my face
place them in the knots
of your bark

crack open my chest
grasp with your branches
my heart
wear it in your hair, a bird house

I am told my heart has a hole
I was born with it
will die because of it
sparrows, though, can
slip through
and live

a condition of love
is fragility, a condition
of fragility is a blind moth
in flight, your leaves
crumpling, or blossoms
stunted by an April snow

When All the Lights Go Out
"Bees are literally worrying themselves to death."
—New York Magazine, June 17, 2015

I don't want grave measures to explore.
Or wild bees to overhear again upsetting rumors about their queen.
The bees, they're dying in mass numbers,
they listen as we debate the fate of our apples and our beans.
Firelight and each night swarms make their way to the beach, again,
without hope or a picture of the future.

Beads of rain strike like anxiety, quickly.
Oh, the bees go colorless and fall from the sky. I know what it's like
to feign belief in my own evolution. As a child,
my grandmother had dreams for me. *Son, you'll be a priest*, you'll see.
But for me, the future was a door cut in the night sky—
                                        nothing on the other side.

Look, see, how the bees enter from the door in the east, like Kamikaze,
buzz over the empty field toward the flames on the beach.
Oh, the gritty spice of smoke riding on the breeze—
I can almost hear the sounds of kids laughing over driftwood crackling.
Why did no one tell them history is taking place?
Why did no one tell them we will all have to pay for it?

Can We Go Back to the Time Before Fire?

Now even the mausoleums
the crypts of martyrs & saints are ablaze.

I ride my bike to the lookout to find a familiar face.
When since the storm
has the air been less see-through?
Not a flake of this falling can be confused with snow.

O apparition, O charred figure,
did you crawl your way from the beach
holding a jar of your teeth & finger nails?
Are you my father?

Grey-eyed boy, teacher's son,
I comb the burning building for you.
A girl gathers the fragments of her mother's bones,
she says you warned that God sends bombs.
They have crowned him in barbed wire, tied him to a fence.

O jaundiced baby, O sister, I cannot sleep either.
I hear your blinking eyes against the pillow,
wings of monarchs brushing the veil
that separates us from the dead.
In the morning, I will take you to shelter.

Turgid holy water, bloodied cassock on the tile floor,
I hold out my tongue & on it
the priest places viaticum—
                            food for the journey
                            take, eat.

Grandma is in the rectory,
she bandages the nuns who refuse to open their eyes.
Sunday, she says, *is the end*
$\qquad\qquad\qquad\qquad$ *of holy waiting.*

If God is a clear window, then what is this siren?
If not a trumpet, then a bushel of orchids
that burst into tears.

O limping dog, O widow, O girl in a wheelchair,
O woman in a red dress...
$\qquad\qquad\qquad\qquad$ Mother? O mother,
running for the bomb shelter—
there will never be enough room for us.

Postlude

At the Site of Jonah's Burial

>*On July 24, 2014, militants with the Islamic State in Iraq and Syria ignited explosives that destroyed the burial site of the prophet Jonah, revered by Christians, Jews and Muslims.*

In the dream, a plume of dust.
Jonah is dead, again—
He leaves only the odor of gunpowder behind.
In the rubble, boys with bombs see a future. We are fleeing
this dry & weary land with no water. In the dream,
Jonah escapes, encased in a pillar of cloud & fire.
In three days, will he reemerge?
Come, sisters, let us go to the sea & sing to our God.
Sing, sisters, sing. Why aren't you singing to the fish?
Jonah, like our mothers, is dead, again.
If the dead in their tombs aren't safe, then not even myth can save us.
At the tree line another fire. Sisters, are you terrified?
No, we are tired. Lord, we are tired of ourselves.
If I were Jonah, I would have stayed in the fish.
In the dream, the plume wasn't dust.
In the dream, Jonah didn't escape.
Sing, sisters, sing. See? The fish are listening.

Loren Moreno is a journalist and writer from Honolulu, Hawaii living in New York City. He is a graduate of the MFA Creative Writing Program at The New School. He is the author of the chapbooks *Aaron & Keoni*, winner of the 2012 Gertrude Press Chapbook Contest, and *At This Late Hour*, awarded runner-up in the 2010 Brickhouse Books Chapbook Contest. His flash and poetry have appeared in *Hawaii Pacific Review, Gertrude, decomP, dogzplot, The American Poetry Journal, JMWW* and more. He has 13 years of experience as an award-winning journalist, working as a reporter for *The Honolulu Advertiser*, contributing editor to HO*NOLULU Magazine*, and an editor at *Adventure Publishing Group*. Loren writes almost exclusively in the chapbook format so much so he created Atomic Theory Micro Press to publish handmade chapbooks by emerging writers.

www.ingramcontent.com/pod-product-compliance
Lightning Source LLC
LaVergne TN
LVHW041505070426
835507LV00012B/1331